Hesed

God's lovingkindness through life and faith

Linda Daruvala

O&U
Onwards & Upwards

Onwards and Upwards Publishers
4 The Old Smithy
London Road
Rockbeare
EX5 2EA
United Kingdom
www.onwardsandupwards.org

First edition, published in the United Kingdom by Onwards and Upwards Publishers Ltd. (2024).

ISBN: 978-1-78815-965-4
Typeface: Sabon LT

To my late parents, Len and Dot,
who first gave me the gift of unconditional love

Endorsements

Poems that usher the sublime into the everyday. They are present and earthy, but with flashes of the another kingdom always breaking in.

Rhidian Brook
Writer and broadcaster

Linda's awareness of the presence and love of God in all things shines through this collection of poetry. An eclectic mix of deeply personal experiences, wonderful observations and beautifully imaginative interpretations of Scripture, 'Hesed' will challenge you if you let it. Savour the poems slowly and they will lead you into your own prayerful encounters with the God who longs to make himself known to you.

Pat Marsh
Author of 'Whispers of Love'

Linda Daruvala is a gifted wordsmith who is not afraid to ask questions through her poetry, both praising and challenging God and the reader, akin to the Psalmist of old. She is not afraid to lay bare her personal emotions. I believe [these poems] will resonate and bring relief to others who face similar difficult experiences...

Reverend Lisa-Claire Holmes
Associate minister
The Ray Valley Benefice, The Diocese of Oxford

These poems powerfully explore the lovingkindness of God in language that is at once immediate and rich with spiritual insight. Whether recalling a Northumbrian 'Poustinia' – the monastic 'desert' of Orthodox Christian tradition ('You are...') – or revelling in the vibrant autumn colours of maples at Bramshott in Hampshire ('Avenue of Maples, Bramshott'), Linda Daruvala's subtle poetic voice illuminates the joys and struggles of the life of faith.

Many of these poems move seamlessly from detailed evocations of a specific place – the "warm smell of old litter" ('The Kench') – towards challenging metaphysical spaces of prayer and "holy fire" ('Fiery John'). Above all, this collection is alive with a homely divinity, a deft balancing of the everyday and the transcendent as the "heart sings by the Jurassic coast" ('Dorset Psalm'). In the midst of the joys and sorrows of these poems, God's presence endures:

In You all things hold together,
Alpha and Omega.

('You are...')

The fundamental message of this collection is one of positivity. God's 'hesed', a lovingkindness towards all creation, promises radical transformation. In 'Forgiveness', Daruvala movingly declares:

Fresh growth overtakes the barren landscape
And we no longer remember it as it was.

Dr Richard Hawtree
Poet and medievalist

Acknowledgements

To faithful God who walks alongside me in good and bad times. You give me the inspiration and incentive to write.

To Luke and Leah at O&U; you steer me so kindly and professionally into publishing. You open the platform for my poetry to be shared with a wider audience.

To my loving family for your continual support, praise and encouragement.

To many dear friends who greatly touch me with your stories of how my poems impact you.

To Lisa, who amazingly commissioned an artwork to accompany my first book, *Selah*, and all who use my poems in their ministry.

To those who have offered me opportunities to perform in public the poetry of my heart and my faith.

About the Author

 Linda grew up in Dorset, and fell in love with poetry while studying Thomas Hardy's poems for O Level. She can still recite some of them! An only child, she has always found solitude a comfortable and creative space to inhabit. She gave her life to the Lord at 18 at teacher training college in Winchester, which is where she also began to write. A love of Jesus, travel, contemplation, quiet, photography and art all enable her to meditate and compose her poetry, reflections and prayers. She is inspired by Ignatian spirituality and new Celtic monasticism, and loves to retreat to 'thin' places throughout the UK, especially Holy Island.

Linda was a primary school teacher and is married to Jung. They live in Surrey and are very proud of their two wonderful adult sons, Pete and Simon. Since being healed from Non Hodgkins Lymphoma in 2010, Linda has particularly relished the fresh blessings and opportunities of each new day.

Linda leads creative workshops in her home church, St Alban's, Hindhead, and at local retreat centres. She sings in her church worship band and gospel choir, and her joy is to spend time at a little rented beach hut on Hayling Island. She loves listening to God, new travels, sunsets, watercolours and baking lemon drizzle cake!

Contents

Forgiveness

Forgiveness is not a new roll of turf
Placed on raw open earth;
A quick fix
To a freshly green verdant lawn,
Pristine and complete.
No, it is grass seed
Generously and deliberately sprinkled,
Widely distributed over all areas of soil,
Gently watered and nurtured,
Till a few shoots appear.
Then green starts to overtake brown
Like dye into water,
Swathes of tiny leaves prising through the loam.
Gradually the tender blades develop and grow
Till the lawn is a mass of soft emerald
With a few bare patches.
Forgiveness is seldom complete,
But in time
Fresh growth overtakes the barren landscape
And we no longer remember it as it was.

*This poem was entered into the South Downs Poetry Festival
Competition 2022: The Binsted Prize, and judged by Naomi
Foyle. It was commended and I was invited to read out
'Forgiveness' at a poetry evening in St Mary's Church, Binsted
on Friday June 10th, 2022.*

Six Weeks

When my son was born
My mum was given weeks to live.
Bed-bound and weak,
We placed the crib by her side
So she could watch this new life;
Her wrinkled hand stroked new skin.
She gazed upon the round blue eyes
As yet unchanged,
His mop of black hair,
Smiling at the movements and noises
Only a newborn makes,
And the deep rhythmic breathing of sleep
That she wished for herself.
He entertained her,
Beginning life as she was ending hers.
He brought a contentment and a peace
To settle and comfort days of pain and deterioration,
A new life emerging as another fades.
She died six weeks later
And at the funeral service the silences
Were interrupted by burps and gurgles.
He was saying goodbye too.
Did he illustrate the hope that there is new life to come after
    this one?
That this was not her end, but a new beginning
With a body that does not suffer or weep
But revels in the freshness and newness

Of life in the heavenly realm?

Stile

I looked into the furrowed field –
Yet another wooden stile
Boundaried by barbed wire;
No other way ahead.
Which foot to put on first?
One hand cupped round the upright,
Swinging over a limp leg
That seems to be stuck in slow motion,
Ungainly, off balance,
Blindly feeling for the plank
That I know is there
But behind my view.
Weight shifted, teetering unsteadily
And then a heavy landing onto solid ground.

Is healing like this, Lord?
An obstacle, a hurdle, needing uncomfortable effort,
Shifting sand when I seek the rock?
Or is it actually
An easily opened gate,
A smooth latch just pushed aside
To enter into a new journey field
Of life, changed perspective, a different horizon?

Lord, if I have to clamber over stiles
Would You hold my hand for balance,
Help me find firm footing?

If this time I can just steadily walk forward
Through the latch gate to a new vista,
May I bless You and be grateful
For Your mercies;
Acknowledge that You are the Gatekeeper
And not the erector of stiles.
Amen.

Lost Craft

I found in lockdown
My late mother's sewing box.
Inside, a smooth wooden mushroom,
A worn small metal loom
With a lever and 12 hooked bars –
The 'Sellars Rapid Darner'.
Does anyone darn any more?
Do you remember how uncomfortable it was?
A hard woollen lump
Right in the place where your big toe meets the tip of your
    boot
Or where your soft heel meets the sole,
Causing blisters or a callous;
An annoying grit that you can't shake out of your shoe.

Friction causes holes
And it's all too easy now to throw the sock away
And toss a new 5-pack pair
Into the supermarket trolley.

We may have holes
In relationships,
Some worn through, or fraying with jagged edges
That will get worse if we don't deal with them.
Do we just as easily throw these away
To pick up new ones?
Or do we work hard to mend and darn

The warp and weft
Of reconciliation?
Or is that a lost craft too?

Fiery John

He didn't wear a beekeeper's suit
So did he get stung?
Or was he like Francis or Cuthbert and
Bees gave up their honey easily?
Did he collect the camel moult himself?
For he had no money to trade, nor the wherewithal to weave
   the cloth.

Perhaps Elizabeth wove it for him.
She would have much preferred him to wear a robe
Like everyone else, but
At least it would be warm
As he wandered in the cold wilderness.
She would have cooked him bread on the fire
With a little olive oil dip, and set out figs and grapes
If he visited home.
But that was rare
For John had a fire in his belly
That required him to live off the land,
Catch and crunch protein-filled locusts
And sweeten his sun-baked lips with honey;
A loner, dressed as a tramp,
Wild, matted hair, trudging along the riverbank
Muttering, self-absorbed, calling out loudly, "Repent!
   Repent!"
Scary to behold him, best avoided,
Especially if you were in soldier's uniform or a priest.

But how his demeanour changed
When someone knelt before him
Asking for forgiveness
And desiring to be baptised;
How his eyes shone and his smile captivated the crowd
As he plunged the sinner into the cold depths of the Jordan
And then raised his arms rejoicing
At another soul saved for the Lord...

Then, as he
Cursed the indignant onlookers for their hypocrisy,
He continued to trudge, sopping wet,
Footprints sliding along the mud and grasses,
Following his call onward
To prepare firm ground for the Saviour,
The One who would indeed baptise with holy fire.

Jesus Blesses the Children

Was it an orderly queue
Like the playground bell,
Or was it a melée,
Excited children gathered around,
Pushing, shoving,
Wanting to be next,
Chattering, laughing as only children can?
Shy veiled mothers looking on, silently
Hoping their child
Would be next embraced,
Would be next blessed,
Would be next held by
These open arms of Jesus.
Did babies sit on His lap
As in many twee images,
Surrounded by birds and rabbits?
It was much more ordinary than that –
Stained sun-scorched faces, ragged clothing,
A warm breeze flapping robes and cloaks,
Dust and dirt enveloping as more folk joined the crowd
To one central point:
Jesus.
The very loving presence of God filtered through
The Son of God
In His adoration
Towards these very young innocents,
Delighting toddlers and infants and parents

(Perhaps even adolescents).
And what did they feel?
Love, warmth, security, purpose?
Did they know this was a once-in-a-lifetime moment
Or just disregard it afterwards
And run off to continue to play?
Which of these children grew up to be followers of The Way?
Which of these children traversed countries to spread the
    message?
Which of these children birthed generations of believers?
God knows –
Because He held each one.

Based on Mark 10:16 (TPT).

I Named Them

We went to a conference,
Talked of loss, miscarriage, stillbirth;
Emotional time...
I have two lovely sons
But I lost three babies,
All at twelve weeks old.
Someone said, 'They might have been girls.'
Some said, 'It's nature's way.'
Some said, 'Try again.'
Some said, 'We'll investigate next time.'
The conference speaker talked of naming,
Of committing these lost ones to God,
So we did.
We worshipped privately, entered a time of prayer;
We thought about these babies;
We thought they were indeed girls
And named them:
Rachel, Esther and Ruth.
We imagined
Rachel with dark hair, brown eyes, beautiful, placid, graceful;
Esther as adventurous, joyful, outgoing, musical;
Ruth as quietly contemplative, serene, gentle, compassionate;
A mix of our personalities through all three.
In a time of communion we committed them to God.
It was a time of tears, releasing, hope and warmth,
That these three were lost to us. But not to God.

You Are...

You are to me, Lord:
The honey embedded in a honeycomb;
The nectar secreted in a flower's depths;
The flash of a yellow tang emerging from coral fronds;
The solo violin in an unfinished symphony;
The final brushstroke in a priceless masterpiece;
The dovetail in an antique cabinet;
The cornerstone of a momentous cathedral;
The iridescent wing of dragonfly hovering above a bullrush;
The snow-capped pinnacle amongst a thousand hills;
The sweet evening melody of a lone blackbird;
The first expressive cry of a newborn babe;
The soft down of a scurrying chick;
The rounded jade stone on Iona's beach;
The crag and castle on Lindisfarne;
The poustinia at Nether Springs;
The runner ducks by bubbling stream at Millhouse;
In You all things hold together,
Alpha and Omega.

A poem describing when I have deeply felt the presence of God, on retreat and in nature.

Rushmoor Lake

Beautiful, beautiful place:
Soft hush of a breeze;
Chirp of songbird, call of coot;
Backlit rushes and tall, slender grasses;
Gently rippling lake, adorned with gleaming floating weed
Yet clearly reflecting the surrounding dark pine and white
  birch.
Dark shadows conceal shoals of carp just playing with the
  fishermen;
Hot warmth of midday sun,
Searing, scorching the dry earthy bank.
Sudden ripple as a snout pokes the surface,
Tempting the hook and bait. Ah, lost it.
Gurgling splash of a mallard awkwardly landing;
Melodic birdsong criss-crossing the valley, mate calling to
  mate;
Burnt-orange winged dragonfly
Alighting delicately on a bending frond;
Shimmering muted reflections of dark branch and faded
  boughs.
Sparkle of movement in the far recesses;
Out of reach for this fisherman's line.
Playful fish, basking lazily in their safety.
Camouflaged rabbit in shade of the bracken;
Clusters of brilliant blue damselflies delicately hovering above
  a nettle
Darting; a glimpse of

Thick, streamlined tadpoles
Hatching near a discarded, upturned sodden wooden chair;
Overgrown moss infiltrating a hidden pathway, curving
    invitingly.
Two carp cruising nonchalantly in the weed-covered lake
    centre
Protected by nature and instinct.
Deep violet rhododendrons in bud.
Whole shoal of black-tailed battleship fish
Following the leader, encircling their territory.
Fox or badger hole, hidden predator
Awaiting the cool of the evening for its supper.
Views of Hankley scarred by military,
A piercing white scoreline among the muted heathers and
    gorse.
Flashes of yellow brimstone butterfly,
Investigates with its proboscis tongue, then flying away to
    oblivion.
Thick, gouged chestnut bark of the pine,
Encrusted, magnificent splendour, wise and experienced;
Gnarled roots of ivy clambering up its old, deceased diseased
    trunk;
Old bark tumbled to the floor, home for ants and autumn
    fungi,
Soft feathery fir waving and fanning like palms along the
    sheltered path.
Disturbed fish, feeling some vibrations, scurry away;
Huge carp are still lingering among the surface weed
Like dolphins' backs emerging elegantly from their depths,
Searching plankton and freedom;

Groups of rudd, together, secure.
Countless pine cones scattered, fallen from above;
Shades of muted browns, beige, earth tones.
Late afternoon dappled reflections like a Paul Klee canvas.

Packing up the rods and lines,
It's been a beautiful day
And it's never all about the fishing!

Overshadowing

When did she know?
Was it when she said to Gabriel,
"May your word to me be fulfilled"?
Was it quiet, unnoticeable
Until she felt sick a few weeks later?
Or did she feel a light movement deep in her womb,
Enough for her to cradle her tummy
Knowing that her holy motherhood had begun?
Or did she feel the most wonderful sensation
Caught up in an overwhelming joy and adrenaline rush
As the very Spirit of God overshadowed her
And birthed new life within her?

You Will Find Him...

Did you know
That newborn lambs from ewes
Specially selected for Passover sacrifice
Were gently wrapped in cloths,
Laid in feeding troughs lined with soft hay,
Protecting them from any hurt? Neither did I.
For the Passover lambs must be unblemished
With no bruising nor broken bones.

"And this will be a sign to you – you will find the babe...
Wrapped in swaddling cloths, lying in a manger..."

Mary simply did it,
The angels declared it,
The shepherds witnessed it,
I am amazed by it;
The Son of God already complicit
In God's plan for mankind
Of salvation.

Ref: Luke 2:12.

The Darkest Hour is Just Before Dawn

I've come to a standstill.
It's so black,
So black.
I can't see any further ahead
Nor indeed where I have come from.
Are there mountains surrounding me
In this indigo valley?
Towering crags snow-iced in winter,
Vertical tumbling joyous waterfalls?
Are there undulating hills flowing with fresh green grass
With sheep grazing lush meadows?
Are there pastel wildflowers strewn around my feet
And a small, quiet stream
To picnic by?
I can see nothing,
Hear nothing,
Feel... nothing.
You say You are with me, Lord;
I can't see, or hear, or feel You?
I've had enough now;
I'll just stay here
In my loneliness and despair.
No further;
This is it.
Then I do feel... something;

A warmth, a body heat against my aching spine.
A strong arm curves around my own limp limb;
It's comforting.
An arm beckons onwards, inviting me on.
I sense some movement;
This person is starting to slowly walk,
Guiding me along in His own momentum.
I relax into this gentle authority of continuing on;
He takes all my weight.
It seems easier to walk with Him at my back, pressing on
And as He alone looks up at the faintest glimmer of an
    emerging sunrise,
He whispers:
"The darkest hour is just before dawn."

Based on Psalm 23:4.

My 17th Birthday

I'm sitting in the corner
Curled up and safe, protected,
But in reality I'm blocked in,
Knowing I'm rejected.

Outside the sixth form common room
Facing nowhere, eyes downcast,
In quiet and dark, my thoughts flood in;
No escape from issues past.

So I'll just sit in my own world,
Observe the fun and games;
Don't make threats or laugh at me,
Don't call me unkind names.

I'm fine in my own company,
I won't be in your way.
Leave me alone within my space;
I'm shy and quiet, can hide away.

Unstreetwise girl, naive and sweet,
Head bowed low and knees tucked in,
Fun and friendships so remote,
How I can sense that child within.

No birthday song or cake or gifts.
Don't notice me, just pass on by;

Won't make a fuss, absorb the taunts,
But out of sight you'd see me cry.

Emerging from this troubled cell,
I unroll gently, reach up high
To the God who rescued me,
For, one year later, heard my cry;

Enveloped me in loving arms
And gave me a new family
Of kind and gentle, caring friends;
Full acceptance finally.

I met my bully once, you know –
School reunion party.
"I don't know why," she said with grace.
"You made it all so easy."

Note: This was written following a drama in which we were asked to place a voluminous scarf over ourselves and sit under it, to block out senses and to hear what God might be saying. Sadly, it reminded me of incidents in my youth when I was badly bullied and had felt isolated, alone and different. I'm glad to say the sensitive leader enabled us to emerge safely and slowly from the wrapping into the light, and with gentle music and creativity, we responded to and dealt with our feelings and allowed freedom to be released. I met this lady again in 2023 at another school reunion and she said sorry. We were able to hug and put it all finally into the past. I think we both felt it had been healed and lifted.

Photini

A parched mouth after an exhausting journey,
Sitting on the well, encountering a woman,
Even with dry tongue and sore lips,
Hoarsely telling the good news,
Answering her questions;
And as her eyes wide opened
To His revelations
Did she then lower her bucket into the well for Him
Or drop her jar, flee back to the village:
"Could this be the Anointed One we have waited for?"
Hopefully, Jesus did get His drink of cool water...
How like Jesus to always put aside His own needs
For the needs of others.

Based on: John 4:7-26: the story of the woman at the well. In the Eastern Orthodox church, this woman is named as Photini – the first woman evangelist.

Sweet Things

I like sweet things…
Dairy Milk chocolate,
Nutty Ferrero Rocher,
Blueberry muffins,
Werther's Originals – sugar free, of course,
Lemon drizzle cake, chocolate cream eclairs,
Decadent golden syrup on my porridge,
But…

The sweetest of all things
Must have been the manna –
Wafers coated in honey
From God's kitchen.

Uprooted

"They've moved the beach huts!" I exclaimed,
Simultaneously leaping from the car with my camera
To look at the bedraggled sight of
An irregular line of pastel huts, now awkwardly positioned,
Neighbours separated, sea views diminished;
'Cloudy Bay' and 'Sea Shack' back to back;
Shabby, forlorn, isolated, abandoned;
Some look much the worse
Jacked up on sleepers, askew, ill placed,
Retreated back from the shore,
Surrounded by 'No Entry' signs and heavy fencing.

The Island is dredging its beach;
Everything pushed back for the machinery,
To swallow and mould shingle
For new groynes, unnatural shelving,
Flood defences before the winter turmoil
(When huts have been known to take a swim!).
Original sites forcefully vacated;
A changed vista, placement, outlook,
Upheaval, disruption, discomfort,
Seemingly in the wrong place, uprooted for the new planning.

I'm talking beach huts here...
But my mind wanders to migrants, Lord,
Caught up in waves of policy that wash them away from
    settlement,

Security, ownership of land,
Establishing a home.
I think of Nauru, Moria, Zaatari,
Sangatte, Brook House, Aylan Kurdi,
Crumpled dinghies, refrigerated vans,
Trafficked people seeking solace, security, a homeland.
Why do authorities have this power
To manipulate belonging,
Sweep aside dignity, ancestry,
Replacement of lives already shattered,
Uprooted from family, careers and settlement?
Pawns taken at the start of a brutal game
And then swept aside by a hand full of money...

Lord, re-establish citizenship and protection
For these souls fleeing for freedom,
That, despite it all,
They place their hands in Yours
And You will still the water.

Hidden Deaths

Each leaf gently flutters down
Onto an already smothered floor of dead leaves:
Another life well lived
Just silently slips away through lack of breath;
Covid creeps in and smothers
And a much-loved relative
Succumbs,
Closes eyes,
And gently passes...
Alone.

Hesed

Strange
How Covid-19
Not only suffocates life breath
But attacks relationship,
Causing us to repel touch,
Flinch from a warm kiss,
Deflect an offered hug.
Interrupts all too brief
Mumbled masked conversations,
Prevents family togetherness,
Celebrations or just 'ordinary time' days
Spent walking, talking, bonding, loving.
This pandemic contradicts our loving God
Who initiated relationship,
Yearns for connection, communication
Within His enveloping lovingkindness.
In this year 2020
Although we have restrained from human touch,
Let us outreach our hands to our Father
Who comforts and heals with His *hesed*.

Kaleidoscope

My eyes gaze on such an ornate,
Magnificent pattern;
Glass gems held in a symmetrical mosaic,
Glowing with brilliant light;
Shapes and colours like a vivid prism rainbow
In a perfectly aligned stained-glass window
Contained within this mini tube.
2019 felt like this...

But then I twisted the kaleidoscope
And everything changed,
Fell apart;
Jewelled shards became dishevelled, scattered,
Collided, separated;
Broken fragments scrunching as a rainstick,
In disarray.
2020 felt like that...

But then a new pattern slowly emerged
Even more beautiful than the last,
Everything again in harmony;
A new design composed of the same elements,
Beautifully, aesthetically glorious;
Bright emeralds, rubies, amber and topaz
To savour, to once again bring joy and pleasure.
2021 feels like this...

Familia

My favourite restaurant overlooks the Solent.
Push the seafront door, buffeted by onshore breeze,
Into the warm ambience of this chic family Italian;
Pristine gingham cloths, mahogany wheelback chairs,
Aroma of parmesan and oregano.
Candlewick lit, rustic campagna bread and herbed olives
    served;
So homely, so inviting, so welcoming.
Come into the Lord's presence
Away from the chills of life
To a comfortable place where you are known,
Your seat reserved,
A sumptuous meal prepared of your favourite dishes...
And your Lord is already there, sitting quietly,
Breaking the bread –
For this is a table for two.

In the Sand

It's fun writing words in the sand;
I've once written 'Holy Island'
With a huge flourish on the 'y'
And an upward curl on the 'd' –
A wonderful memory of a treasured time.
Jesus once wrote in the sand
As angry accusers prepared to stone an unfortunate,
A woman bereft of love, dignity and protection.
She stands there
Exposed as if naked,
An unyielded innocence,
Victim of a man's lust
Regarded as an unfaithful harlot;
Deserving of such harsh ordained punishment
By the righteously upright few
Who also thrust an accusatory question to the Rabbi.
Jesus walks up to her
And looks at this downcast child of God,
Shame and fear etched in her soft-skinned face.
He crouches and writes with His finger in the sand
His name: 'Jesus'.
Her lowered eyes see His name,
She knows it means 'Saviour'.
Yes, child, your Saviour is here beside you now.
Jesus indeed stands and looks out at the hard hearts.
He faces the crowd alongside her;
They are together in this.

Jesus says His answer
And the begrudging onlookers squirm away.
She hears the heavy thuds of the stones
Dropping on the sand
And she lingers on His name
Written in the sand.
Your Saviour, child, stands beside you
With all you face today.
Lift your head and take courage;
Look with Him at your fears, your challenges, your past.
Jesus is with you;
You are not alone
No matter what.

Based on John 8:1-11.

Comprehension

Read the passage and answer the following questions:
1. Who is God?
2. What am I here for?
3. What happens when I die?

Oh, dear Lord,
Sometimes I read both Testaments and
Don't understand at all.
My mind swirls like ripple in ice cream;
I strain to comprehend
A magnanimous God
Who has the whole world in His hands,
Who sees you in your small corner and I in mine,
Who's gotta home for me in Gloryland that outshines the sun.
Is this doubt?
Is this unbelief?
Is this just pressing in to want to know more?
My human mind
That weighs just three pounds –
About the same as this laptop –
Wrestles with grasping key questions of faith.
It feels like showing my cat a map of the world and
Describing New York, Ayers Rock, polar bears,
When all she knows is our garden and the food bowl;
Like catching a butterfly between my hands
Which is an impossibility in itself,

But in doing so
Would hide the very beauty I hoped to observe;
Like placing a magnifying glass on one petal of Monet's
    waterlilies
To peer at the colour, the strokes,
But unable to see I am surrounded by
Monumental canvases of violet-blue reflections;
Or that I might stroll through Giverny?
The answer to all three questions is already known –
It's Jesus, of course –
But it seems too simple to write.
I need to explain my answer
In no more than 300 words.
Oh, dear Lord,
I so much prefer Creative Writing –
But that's on Thursday.

The Four Commons Walk, in November

God used His watercolours today:
A bright blue azure wash streaks across the smooth paper,
Smudged white clouds for contrast,
Joy and delight in His exuberance and pleasure
Of a sun-soaked autumn day.
So much fun splashing and dripping colours in a Jean Haines*
    way,
Splattering siennas, ochres and umbers,
Evergreens, russets and fawns.
His soaked brushes touch the tops of the trees;
Colours cascade down the fluttering leaves
And puddle on the woodland floor.
Light swift strokes of branches and twigs,
Thin silver birch candles with vivid yellow flames,
Delicate golden filigree of illuminated bracken.
He uses 'Daniel Smith†' metallics
To shimmer the copper boughs
And glisten the red oak.
Natural pigments seep the warm brown beech;
Bright red and candy pink droplets as
Bountiful berries upon the holly and spindle;
A foreground of faded fly agarics
With their popcorn beads and lace petticoats;
And there, do you see, just tucked by the log,
He carefully places an upright lone silver grey squirrel,

Devouring an acorn in its cupped paws,
Who then turns and looks to the painter
As though waiting for the Creator to finish
Yet another masterpiece.

Note: This is a most beautiful six-mile walk through four connecting Surrey commons – Witley, Rodborough, Milford and Thursley – protected natural woodland and heathland.

* Jean Haines is an inspirational watercolour artist: www.jeanhaines.com.

† Daniel Smith is a manufacturer of quality watercolour paints, endorsed by Jean Haines: www.danielsmith.com.

Spring Harvest, Minehead AD33

Well, that was quite some conference;
Just one guy, fairly unknown
But with a reputation!
Sitting far away from the Big Top,
Just healing all who came.
Word spread around the chalets,
Dining areas emptied,
Seminars cancelled,
Worship bands left in solitary,
As all sat by the beachside
Watching as one after another –
The blind, the deaf, the paralysed,
The depressed, the amputees, the cancer-stricken –
Were all touched and immediately healed.
For three whole days
This young empathetic, energetic man
Proclaimed compassion and love, acceptance and hope
To those searching for the truth.
Courage grew, and the meek, the sceptical and downright
    atheist
Offered their burden to this Jesus
And received all they had ever hoped for.
No one attended the late night films
Or browsed the bookstalls;
New WWJD T-shirts forgotten on their beds,

Ferris wheel tickets discarded.
Early every sunrise morning
Till late every moonlit starry night
They came and listened and were healed.
Three days later it was time to end;
The young man left and people dispersed
To feed on fish and chips,
To flood into the venues singing praise and adoration
As never before,
Streamed new songs of worship,
Created gigantic canvases of ethereal art,
Silences amid murmured conversations,
Some laying hands on others,
Some walking into town to reach out to locals
To heal as they had been healed.
Do you think he'll come to Skegness?

Based on Matthew 15:31.

Unnamed Colours

I love paint charts.
Not that I like decorating,
But I peruse the images of colours presented to me:
Subtle shades, tints, hues, tones;
A quilt of patches ready to be sewn together.
As I immerse myself in a mesmerising sunset
Or delicate hydrangea petals
Or a wild Cornish ocean,
I struggle to describe accurately the colours I feel;
I search the paint charts with intensity
And find
Moon Yellow alongside Pineapple,
Lemonade with Masala,
Scallop Shell by Frosted Almond.
Everyday colours journey into new realms with their
    neighbours.
I seek the end of my pilgrimage to thus discover
My perfect adjectives;
I infuse the given names with delight.

Though, whenever I paint with watercolours,
Such exquisite ethereal blends flow
That I feel they must be left unnamed.

As words rise up within me
To capture a beautiful scene
Or a God-given glimpse of awe,

Wonder or praise,
A heartbeat, breathtaking moment
That I want to hold on to,
Not rush away from,
When all is still
And heaven and earth meet –
I cannot describe those either;
They too are left unnamed.

Depression

I just sat there
Totally disengaged
While Jung* built sandcastles with the boys,
Digging furrows and channels
Which the boys gleefully filled with overflowing buckets from
the sea;
Tunnels and turrets with paper flags, bridges and shell
windows.
It was a hot day on this Welsh beach,
Wearing my purple swimsuit,
Backed by the black rock cove,
Looking out but not focused on anything;
Not tired but lethargic,
Not exhausted but lacking energy,
Not active but apathetic,
No joy, no pleasure, no delight;
Every interaction a demand,
Every meal a chore,
Every walk a marathon,
Every exposure a judgement,
Every conversation veiled.
That heavy cloud weighing me down,
So tangible I couldn't lift my head;
All I could see was me
Shrouded, chained, entangled, limp,
Of no use, a failure, a disappointment.
But one day there was a worship song†:

"When my world was falling apart
Your golden breath took darkness away.
If I ask, You won't let me go…"
As I listened I cried, and as I cried I listened
To those penetrating words
Of a lone candle still flickering,
Of a love that does not let me go,
A promise of wonderful days;
A gentle voice
That changes my wrong perceptions,
That counteracts lies with truth,
That strengthens my weakness;
His gentle voice in the stillness,
Guiding, directing, leading
From despair to joy,
From confusion to clarity,
From waste to beauty;
"Flowerless trees blooming carefree",
Frozen streams melting,
Broken games lovingly mended.
And it lifted.
Just like that.
That afternoon I offered to cook the meal
At the youth hostel;
Chose the ingredients,
Enjoyed the kitchen,
Prepared a Martha meal for my family
And became the 'me' again
That was always there
But attacked and hidden by this cloud

That seems to move over whoever and whenever and wherever
 it likes,
Hovers and penetrates
Until it reaches that point when the Saviour says,
"ENOUGH!"
And I and you and they know available freedom.

Jung is my husband.

†*The worship song is by Moya Brennan called 'Where I stand'
taken from the album 'Whisper to the Wild Water' (1999).
Songwriters: Tim Jarvis / Moya Brennan; Where I Stand lyrics
© Universal Music Publishing Mgb Ltd. Once at Spring
Harvest, I went along to Moya's evening performance and was
able to tell her (very emotionally I might add!) that it was her
song that brought me out of depression. I hugged her and
thanked her. She probably thought I was unhinged!*

Prayer

We bend our knees and close our hands
And bow to One who understands.
We praise, we seek, we ask, we plead
To One who knows our every need.
God, do You answer every prayer
Or do You stand aloof out there?
We enter into holy ground
Where Your heartbeat may be found,
Pour out to You what's causing pain;
Yes, it's me, Lord, here again.
Where are You, Lord, exactly though?
Within, without, above, below?
Do You see me kneeling here
Under burdens I can't bear?
I'm looking up to You, O Lord,
Craving promises from Your Word.
You say You see me here, Your child,
My problems can be rectified;
You're saying Grace, Compassion, Comfort, Love
Stream like sunbeams from above.
Jesus, to You, my Saviour King,
This day my life I'm offering.

Jochebed – Mother of Moses

How often she would recall those last few hours
Feeding him for the last time,
Gazing down at his baby face,
His huge eyes looking adoringly, completely focussed entirely
    on her;
A fierce maternal bond that she would never have yielded
Yet has to be separated for his own safety.
As they make their way to the Nile –
Cautiously at midday, the woman's hour, veiled faces in dark
    scarves,
Gently, quietly, with hurry without haste,
Casually, avoiding attention –
They approach the beauty of the azure river
On this sunlit day when hearts are clouded with fear and
    terror.
A well fed child is contentedly asleep
Amongst the soft linen cloths she has so lovingly swaddled
    around him
In the tar-blackened handwoven basket.
She pauses at the rushes, kneels and scours the bank,
Searching for the perfect place
Where the current would not disturb,
Where the stalks are at their thickest,
Where the ledge is level and firm.
There's a tiny inlet she can reach and tuck in the basket tightly
Just as she has tucked Moses into his cradle so many times.
She savours the final kiss on his tiny forehead,

She considers, and pushes the basket over a little more to the
    left;
It is secure now.
She murmurs a prayer and offers her child, not to the river
But to the God of Israel who is her only hope.
She does not see and is completely unaware
Of a figure hidden around the curve of the river
Watching her, nudging her mind and spirit,
Ensuring she finds the perfect place to abandon her child.
It is Jesus, waist deep in the water,
His silent words directing her thoughts.
And as she leaves, weeping, and ascends the bank to return to
    her house
(For this is no longer a home without the cry of her baby),
No basket, no daughter, no son,
So Jesus too ascends the opposite bank, muddy robes dripping
As the tears in His eyes for her wretched sorrow.
She had found listening to Him so easy when they dreamed the
    plan together,
And now it is reality;
She has heard Him again at this crucial moment.
He knows that all is now in place
For Moses to be found, protected, nurtured in luxury
And to be then raised up for God's own people to be set free;
This placement had to be perfect,
This strange strategy accomplished.
God is raging against the evil rampaging through His people;
He uses the unusual and seemingly downright dangerous
To fulfil His plan.

And do you know He prepares a perfect place and time for
   you
To be found and rescued
Just as He did for Moses?

Trust

Jesus faced with death:
A wrapped body lain in a tomb
Sealed with a stone;
Lazarus is dead.
Jesus weeps,
Shudders with emotion,
The realisation
This is the miracle sign
God has prepared to show Him.
He thanks the Father,
Trusts His power;
Lazarus staggers out
Into life
As will Jesus
In a few weeks' time.

Butterflies in the Meadow

Used to be the sheep field –
Small flock of Jacobs
With cappuccino fleece;
We'd take the boys, watch and count the twin lambs.
Now a wilding meadow,
Sweeping wheaten grasses,
Yellow ragwort and plantain
Colonised daily by
Pencil-long dragonflies,
Mesmerising butterflies –
Orange tip, meadow brown,
Cabbage-white wings sunlit
Like ultraviolet in a '70s disco.
Just a week of life
Energetically feeding, building up a body
Ready to produce eggs
For a future generation;
A passion week fraught with predators
But with the overriding instinct to reach the perfect timing
To lay, then die.
As did Jesus;
A Passion week fraught with predators
But with the overriding instinct to reach the perfect timing
To bow His head and die
For past, present and future generations.

Joseph of Arimathea

Did you have a dream?
A forewarning or premonition
That your pristine tomb would be needed by Christ?
Did God tell you to go to the foot of the Cross,
Ask for the limp body
And that the request would be granted?
Or had you and Nicodemus already hatched the plan
To immediately manipulate an ashamed Pilate
To offer to remove this embarrassment
To persuade him to let Jesus go
Out of sight, out of mind?
Were the linen cloths a last minute scurry
Or were they prepared at a secret location
And the fragrant spices already mixed in a jar alongside?
Was it an impetuous commitment of love and grief to
Bring Jesus to the safety and security of your own new tomb
Hewn by skilled craftsmen in a verdant garden?
Or did you trust an angel who had declared to you
It is only borrowed for three days?
Joseph, you showed the greatest compassion of all followers.
You carried the body of our Lord gently, tenderly and
    courageously
With reverent dignity and honour
To a clean place of burial
And indeed, three days later,
The site of God's magnificent resurrection power.
Did you witness the discarded cloths?

Could you feel God's presence inside?
Joseph, were you eventually buried there?

Resurrection Angel

He simply sat on top of it!
A job well done – it was easily shifted,
Like a competent furniture remover,
A massive stone rolled away
With an effortless shove
Amidst, of course, some lightning and earth tremors for effect;
This was a pivotal moment after all.
Brightening the dawn,
Dazzling the women,
Paralysing the guards,
The stone rolled away. Not for Jesus though –
He is already walking to Galilee –
But for followers to see,
For us to see...
"Come inside," he says.
"Run and tell the others," he says.
He gives the Lord's message:
"I am going ahead... meet me there."
Then he stayed sitting on top of that stone
Just for a while longer,
Alone this time,
Observing the whole scene.
And with a knowing nod,
He slid down, peeped inside for a final look
At the place which had sealed his Lord,
Gave a victorious broad smile...
And left the tomb open

For followers to see,
For us to see...

Based on Matthew 28:1-8.

Note: I know someone who became a Christian at the Garden Tomb in Jerusalem. As she sat looking, she realised that Jesus was not buried there as in the many other tombs she had visited of famous people. He had indeed risen. This tomb was empty.

Those Moments

Those moments when
All around you melts away
Like a Salvador Dali painting,
When all else fades out of focus
And it's just you and God,
His finger touching yours,
His breath warm on your cheek;
His whisper shouts from the heavens
But only you can hear.
Sometimes it happens in worship,
Sometimes it happens within prayer,
Sometimes with a verse of Scripture,
Sometimes a direct word of knowledge.

I remember a young girl
Humbly, gently offering
That God wanted to heal someone with verrucas.
That was one of those moments.
Those words reached my heart, my mind, my skin;
It was for me.
The podiatrist said it was the worst case she'd ever seen –
Unsightly warts all over my hands and feet.
We had tried creams and acids to no avail
But this young girl declared words of healing.
No showmanship,
Just those few quiet words
And I went forward.

She smiled and was relieved.
I felt her relief.
She had wondered whether God had revealed to her
Veruccas or Veronica!
This young girl laid her hands on my feet and prayed
For complete healing in Jesus' name.

No immediate change –
But then, we know miracles don't always work like that.
But a few days later, I was being anointed
For a new season of Christian work
And as I opened my palms to receive blessing
There were no warts.
Not one.
No scars.
Likewise on my feet,
No swelling, soreness, ugly red growths.
Just clear smooth skin.

That moment I know God healed me
I am in awe,
And I treasure that and other moments
When God is tangible and real;
No doubts, no arguments, no separation,
Just Him and I in focus together.

Sunset Hour at Emsworth

I

So amazingly peaceful:
Glory of the setting sun – a golden bronze
Reflected in the shallows of the pebbled shoreline;
Wading seabirds and gulls gliding effortlessly in this minimal
    current,
Silhouettes of graceful swans, stooping to drink and then
    continue
Towards deeper water.
Even the gull cries are restful and pleasant to the ear,
Not squawking
But just a few toots and chirps from bobbing coots.
The lone bark of a solitary dog.
Scrunching footsteps on the shingle;
Admirers walk along the pier to wait and watch
For the last copper rays.
An ungainly duck,
Watery flapping of wings as it lifts to soar
Into the cream-stroked azure sky.
What peace!
A pinkish hue descends like a mist;
Each boat still, content,
Illuminated by a sparkling glow,
The end of an evening.

II

The sunset bursts forth from its contained horizon;
Streaks of crimson, rose, scarlet, salmon and dusk.
Grey silhouette of the Spinnaker,
A few isolated lights;
The regular balustrades of a pier;
Tide out, dappled pink and blue reflections
Of the watercolour sky;
A lightning break of an aeroplane heading south;
Trees seem aflame as a forest fire;
Pastel colours like a baby's bedroom –
Soothing, calm, gentle and soft;
A blanket of bonfire red settles over the view.
Church bells ring muffled against the quiet.
A relaxed new silver moon in its rocking chair,
The only sharpness in this gentle evening.
A smudged sky above an exposed beach,
Vulnerable yet ethereal.

III

This sunset sweeps across the sky
Like a Monet masterpiece,
Intense and invasive,
Overpowering all cottages and boats in a rose haze,
Ever increasing and spreading
Deepening hues of fuchsia and flame,
Layers of magenta, violet and sage;
So beautifully luminescent,
Settling into the raspberry ice cream of puddles;
Wisps of maroon and silver,

Angel hair and wings
Flying above the furnace
Even more,
Scattering rose petals and orange lanterns to splash beneath.

What beauty in an hour;
Who sees it?
God and me
And a few others
Who ponder it and it touches their heart
In a way we cannot respond
Without worship.

10th February, 2008; 4.50-5.50 pm.

He Got What He Asked For

Always been attracted to YouTube fairy lights in the desert.
Rhythmic neon tantalised his senses, mesmerised his thoughts,
   hypnotised his wisdom.
Googled luxury hotels, influencer-led boutiques, illusory
   jackpots –
And now, £5M on his contactless.

He got what he asked for.
First class flight to Las Vegas;
Handled unfamiliar chips in casinos,
Elated by sensual lap dances,
Treated attractive attentive friends to vintage champagne,
Tipped extravagantly in Michelin restaurants,
Till…
His card was declined, out of bucks,
'NO FUNDS AVAILABLE'.
No handouts –
Needed to find a job.
No CV, no 'word of mouth' contacts.

He got what he asked for.
Cleaning streets overnight of vomit, urine, rotten food, rats;
Demeaning minimum wage.
Slept on cardboard he'd found on the streets;
Stank of dirty clothes, unwashed body odour;
Sank into sordid squalor,
Mind-numbing drugs and daytime alcohol.

Soup kitchen server said he should go home;
Kindly counsellor said he had a family.
Showered in the homeless centre,
Sold his body to quickly raise money.

He got what he asked for.
Overnight standby flight to Stansted,
Freshened up at the airport,
Hitched motorway rides.
CCTV clocked him shoeless at the electric gates.
Hung his head, prepared words for the buzzer's response:
"Hello…"

Gates, oh so slowly, creaking open.
Father running.
Son collapsing.
Father embracing.
Son stuttering.
Father weeping.
Son weeping.
"You're home, son."
Servants bringing a wheelchair;
Chef cooking rib eye steak.

Mother runs the bath,
Warms the soft towel,
Wipes the dried blood,
Washes the knotted hair;
Soothing and loving and affirming and grateful,

Her son sleeping heavily now, as innocent as he was when a
  boy.

He got what he asked for.
Forgiveness, acceptance and belonging.

Be careful what you ask for.

Based on Luke 15:11-24, the story of the Prodigal Son.

Avenue of Maples*, Bramshott

Each leaf a poppy; blood red, lifeless,
Strewn along the avenue,
Isolated, scattered;
A killing field.
Yet these Canadians succumbed to pandemic,
A travesty of First World War courage,
To linger and die
In a foreign land
With no hope of returning
To their Maple flag.
Children and adults enjoy the fallen leaves,
Selfies through the sunshine,
Collecting stars of autumn colours –
Crimson, vermillion, flame and gold
Floating from the silver branches –
A collection of nature's medals,
Each owed to the young men
Who gave their lives
Quietly in hospital beds
As did their nursing sister
In 1919.

Canadian Armed Forces Memorial: Many Canadian service-
men were based in Bramshott. The original maple trees were
felled as unsafe in the 1980s but have been replaced by 400
trees, each twinned with a grave in a nearby Commonwealth
War Graves churchyard.

Twixt Times

I don't usually walk in December rain
But it's that week twixt Christmas and New Year;
Needing fresh air, exercise, despite the gloomy forecast;
Every squelch a sole imprint
Into the slimy murky greyness of the claggy woodland path.
But how the rain has drenched these winter woods
With birch bark a crème caramel, spread with clotted cream
And the beech a rich burnished tan with drenched leaves
    looking like
Sleeping bats hanging perilously by their claws,
Twigs marvellously festooned with fairy lights raindrops,
Holly polished to an evergreen gloss shine
Dotted with abandoned red berry beads;
Vivid lime moss scrambles up isolated stumps, crawls along
    chunky roots
And hides under gleaming golden bracken.
But then the weather changes, suddenly colder now,
A driving sleet against me, twixt rain and snow.
My nose runs, my knees feel damp, my hood drips;
Time to head back for hot tea.
I don't usually walk in the rain
But today I have seen these woods twixt winter and spring,
Water saturated, waiting for warmth,
And expectant delight of nesting birds, fox cubs, wild
    primroses.
Lord, where are You in the 'twixt' times?
Should I often rush from one promised season to the next,

Only exploring on sunny, pleasant days?
Or should I stroll and be immersed in some lingering
   discomfort
To experience and understand the preparation
Of all that needs to happen to energise new life, new growth,
   new vision?
Should I seek to loiter more in the here and now, the present,
   the day to day?
For the twixt times are for composing, editing and devising
   Your plans.
May I sense You in them, Lord, even in the uncomfortable
And not always be a fair weather follower.

Rhoda

Why are young people not listened to?

Rhoda running enthusiastically,
Explaining in her exuberance that "Peter is outside the door!"
Disregarded, dismissed by those who know better
Who are still sitting with heads sunk in their hands seeking
    answered prayer,
No time or concern for this excitable young woman.

Our young people, name-called and upskirted, silently groped,
Revenge porn shamed by so called friends and peers;
Coerced online; innocence groomed by manipulators;
Party plied with drink, drugs, to destroy self-esteem;
Confused by their sexuality, regretted lost virginity, constant
    profanity;
Bombarded persistently by perfect faces, body images
    impossible to attain,
Following cyber influencers immorally grasping their loyalty,
Just searching for a love to escape violent, unstable, abusive
    homes

Why are young people not listened to?

Do they once try, and get rebuffed?
Are they ignored as silly, unbelievable, ridiculous liars?
If just once, they should choose you to open up to
At the right time, right place for them

(But maybe not for you),
Just stop, wait and support.
They need you to listen.
Just once.
That all it takes.

And their door will then be opened...

Based on Acts 12:13-15.

Punctuation

An ellipsis just has three dots... a cliffhanger, wait and see.
A lot can happen in three days, a death to life body
From one who has been crucified, in a bracketed dark tomb.
(Encased in a parenthesis) it all seems doom and gloom.
But this hyphenated God-man now walks and cooks and eats.
As all His followers believe, a colon lists His greets:
A resurrected Jesus!!! His disciples become quite bold;
No amount of exclamation marks has ever been foretold.
Sometimes it is good to pause and take time to reflect;
A comma comes in handy here, just silently expect
A change, a new insight, a thought or word or deed;
Perhaps a question mark may be a necessity?
If you feel there's something missing or don't know whose you
    are,
You'll be needing an apostrophe to point out such a care;
People do misuse them, in plurals, leave them out.
If you use them wisely, your heart will have no doubt
Just who you do belong to and fills that missing gap;
Let Jesus be your Saviour, and there's no full stop with that

Justus

That knot tightened deeper in your gut.
The runner up;
Not only that, but there was only a choice of two.
You were so close –
Loved, admired, valued,
But they chose the other one instead.
Why did the lots fall that way?
Did they see a hidden sin or misdemeanour,
Something you're unaware of,
Lacked forgiveness for?
Weren't they confident of your ability, loyalty, courage?
Or was that really God's own choice,
The outcome of loaded dice?
You didn't quite make the cut
When push came to shove;
Just didn't make the grade.
But accepted graciously,
Politely congratulated Matthias,
Despite the sinking feeling in your stomach
Suffocating your words,
Straining your smile.
Only when you're home do you actually
Lower your head downcast in prayer
To wallow in self-pity a bit,
Yet decide to persevere onward
And put this decision day in the past.
We've all been there,

Not selected for the thing we thought we were perfect for;
Watching a touchable dream just fading away,
Dismissed,
Disappointed,
Disillusioned,
Depressed.
You're Just Us.

But you give us hope,
For although you're acknowledged as the 'not chosen',
Facing an unseen future, independent of an apostle's call,
In your unsought freedom you became
Bishop to the City of the Free.
That's ironic, isn't it...

Based on Acts 1:21-26.

Bucket List

When my hair has turned to grey, I'll dye it aqua blue.
I'm not growing old gracefully; there's so much left to do.
Wing walk on an aeroplane, climb Sydney Harbour Bridge,
Marvel the Grand Canyon, see Machu Pichu's ridge,
Hanami under blossoms, revisit Galilee,
Braid my hair at festivals, paint at Giverny,
Sip manhattans in Manhattan, a cream tea at the Ritz,
Gaze Icelandic Northern lights, a llama trek – no spits!
Glissando Celtic harp strings, cycle Amsterdam canals,
Pick some homegrown runner beans, watch breaching
    Southern whales,
Be starry-eyed at Kielder nights in their observatory,
Sing at Grayshott Folk Club, wear tartan at a ceilidh,
Indulge the 1920s on the Orient Express,
Stay long-term down in Dorset for reflection and for rest,
Watch autumn in New England – the maples all in leaf –
Swim with friendly dolphins, snorkel rainbow coral reef,
Eat an oyster, drink Guinness in Dublin, sail over the sea to
    Skye,
See all my friends in person from Canada to Brunei.
That's not very spiritual; you're probably not impressed.
What about reading all those exegesis texts?
Your Matthew Henry commentary, your Bible reading plan?
All those books upon your shelf – Philip Yancey, Henri
    Nouwen?
Just make the most of every day, plan opportunities;
Only then will your bucket list become realities.

You'll maybe not achieve them all but some you can, no
    doubt;
Expensive trips are really not what it's all about.
It's finding out your Ikigai and push that open door.
Oh yes – swim Marina Sands infinity pool in downtown
    Singapore!

Except, Accept, Expect

Yes, for others except for me.
You cannot accept me.
I do not expect You to forgive me.
You say You died for all,
But I am an exception;
I cannot believe
And accept You as my Lord.
Do You expect me to come to You
With my scrap of faith,
Ashamed of all I've done?
I have no excuses, I made my own choices,
Except when I was manipulated.
I'm unaccepted by society,
Grew up in a dysfunctional family;
What do You expect?
I don't trust their religious words,
Except there's just something in Your simple words
That I could accept:
That 'God so loved the world that He gave His only Son
That whoever believes in Him should have eternal life.'
I don't expect anything to happen, but
Okay God, if You're really there,
Accept me as I am.

Based on hearing an Alpha Course testimony.

Reconciliation

I saw the Lord's face –
Beautiful, authoritative,
Ready to speak,
But this time He didn't use words.
He lowered both His arms
And cupped His hands around the heads
Of two children
Who were apart.
He slowly, gently, tenderly drew them together
In front of Him
And within Him
For reconciliation.

Final Call

Arriving at Departures, I slam the taxi door,
Search the flights board, check the time, across the crowded
floor.
"Your booking's all in order; your passport is intact.
I see you have no luggage; I quite concur with that."
Last possessions on the tray, they disappear from sight;
Green light comes on. "Just walk on through, we're calling for
your flight."
Strolling past Earth's Duty Free – its glamour, shine and glitz –
For old time's sake and sheer delight, I spray on Chanel spritz.
I'm driven to the stairway, a chauffeured VIP.
"Take off your shoes; it's holy ground," the driver whispers
me.
A haloed flight attendant smiles a "Welcome to First Class" –
Seat 1A, the best on board, reserved for me at last.
The pilot comes out, hugs me tightly. "We're so glad you
came."
Do captains usually do that? He even knows my name!
There is no safety briefing, lifejacket, oxygen, chute,
Just a perfectly smooth take off on his old familiar route.
"Recline your seat, and close your eyes or watch the DVD.
We've edited the highlights, but we've loved your whole
story."
Soft and fluffy slippers, pyjamas long and white;
I see my name embroidered on a hand palm on top right.
A neatly folded linen cloth is placed upon my lap.
Unleavened bread is shared by all; we spontaneously clap.

They serve me vintage wine drawn out from stone jars long
    ago
And Michelin-starred manna, quail and Eden's fruit fresh
    grown.
A brief and perfect journey, through promised rainbows
    bright,
All passengers illumined by a holy piercing light.
Emerging from the cabin, I feel alive and free,
Soon cartwheeling on soft pink sand alongside turquoise sea.
Why choose a budget airline or sail to seas unknown?
It's Apex-booked and Amex-paid and granted as your own.
O grave, where is thy victory; O death, where is thy sting?
Come thou kingdom citizen, prepare to meet thy King.

I Will Take You Where I Am

On my day of death
Jesus will take my hand
And I will be led to where He is,
And when I arrive,
Like Maria on the Salzburg mountaintops,
Surrounded by a flourishing alpine meadow
In the crisp air,
Where hills disappear into the pale distance,
I will freewheel and sing, "I am Alive!"

There He will stand
And I will approach Him,
Gaze into His face for real,
That face I have many times sought
And occasionally seen in my mind,
Feeling a peace and joy that is beyond that ever felt in the
    world –
A harmony, symphony that creation is one
And I am blessed to be in it;
Spring growth and summer bloom,
No autumn decay or winter sleep,
A brightness that doesn't dazzle the eye,
A warmth that doesn't scorch the skin,
An almost weightless tread,
Grace and beauty in every movement,
An adrenaline rush that sends me dizzy,
Body, mind and spirit aligned,

Freedom to be who I was always called to be
Without the nets of earthly entanglement
Or oppression from the depths.
My voice joins with the blackbird and robin
In sheer delight to be here.
When my time comes, Lord,
Take me to where You are;
That's where I long to be.

Free Play

Remember those days of 'free play'?
There were toys at every shelf height,
A cushioned cosy corner with picture books on a soft rug,
Weighing scales with conkers, marbles, peas and shells,
Old stained easels with huge ivory sheets of paper,
Opaque lidded tubs of musty paints and stumpy brushes,
Plasticene and play dough to squeeze and mould,
A sand tray with plastic sieves, buckets and spades,
A water tray to trickle your hands through, pour, splash, drip
    and drizzle.
God has a playroom of prayer here
To explore and delight in –
Our choice of what we do,
Our choice of how long we spend
By the dwarf fruit tree with dangling leaves,
Each one ready to fall at its appointed time;
The bird bath filled to the brim gently rippled by the warm
    breeze;
Barely budded twigs casting delicate shadows on the sunlit
    moss;
Bright pink fuchsia dancing joyfully, flowerhead bouncing on
    its stems;
Scented leaves of rosemary, bay and sage stroked, rubbed and
    smelt;
A stark cross with pebbles placed underneath,
Each stone a prayer or burden or name;
Painted hearts, glass nuggets, twined twig crosses,

A colourful ceramic butterfly – new life and hope.
Come, spend time playing in this garden prayer room.
You can choose what to do,
You can choose how long you spend
Before you move on.
Explore, delight, enjoy, interact, contemplate.
Your God is here.

Note: Written in the grounds of The Greenhouse Christian Centre, Poole.

Close the Door

Early morning.
A grey, muffled sky;
Trees modelling this year's autumn fashion,
Gently waving like palm wallahs in searing Indian heat.
Tiny goldfinches flitting,
Traversing the garden from one feeder to the next.
Blackbirds swooping onto the plentiful luscious holly berries.
The blossoming viburnum splashes the scene
With pearlescent pink butterflies,
Last of the Bramleys positioned like billiard balls on the leaf-
    strewn lawn.

I close the door,
Light the scented candle
And prepare to enter even more into His presence.

Celtic morning prayer:
"One thing I have asked of the Lord,
This is what I seek:
That I may dwell in the house of the Lord,
All the days of my life;
To behold the beauty of the Lord..."*

A psalm, OT and NT from my fragile, well-thumbed old NIV,
Underlined, highlighted, bookmarks, pressed flowers,
Dried olive leaves from Gethsemane;
Then my own study from the newly fresh Passion Translation,

Re-reading familiar scriptures in exuberant neon colours of
   imagination.

Praying for others: names, concerns, blessings,
Giving hope to despair, joy to mourning,
Comfort to anxiety, healing to dis-ease,
Listening to Him; pictures, words, direction, peace.

"This day be within and without me,
Lowly and meek yet all-powerful...
Christ as a light; Christ as a shield;
Christ beside me on my left and my right."*†

I put away the books, remove my glasses, snuff the candle
And open the door,
Ready to face my day and this world,
Knowing I have been in the presence of Jesus
And that He is with me today
Wherever He may send me.

Based on Matthew 6:6. (My own quiet time in my own room.)

* *Taken from Morning Prayer from the Northumbrian Community's 'Celtic Daily Prayer' published by Collins. Used with permission.*

† *By St Patrick, adapt. by J. Michael Talbot.*

Listening

Do we let others finish
What they are saying
Or are we too keen to
Interrupt with our own agenda?
Dixi.

NB. Dixi, a Latin expression, literally translates as, "I have spoken." When used, it usually means, "I have said all that I had to say." (en.wikipedia.org)

I first discovered this word in the book 'A Christmas Mystery' by Jostein Gaarder.

When God Says No

It's strange when God says no;
Especially when it's a great Christian idea that you've had.
I wanted to go overseas, to be a missionary,
Well, teaching children of missionaries to be exact.
Ever since I was ten
I had been entranced by foreign lands,
Filled Smartie tubes with sixpences for the Leprosy Mission,
Sold booklets of Sunny Smiles faces,
And now I was available.
I was professional,
I was adventurous,
I was in my twenties;
Perfect timing, so I thought.
But I was not to be a missionary;
My applications halted in negative replies.
I did go overseas but as a teacher
For a large oil company.
I travelled all over Asia, far and wide
And fell in love with Thailand,
Felt drawn to the children, the language, the beauty, the food.
Ah, this is why I've come,
A step nearer my missionary idea –
But before I could investigate further
I fell in love with Jung*,
Completely, overwhelmingly,
And he with me.
I guess God knew me better.

He said no to my own missionary call;
He didn't see me on my own amongst the hill tribes,
He saw me mothering a loving family here.
Strange that God said no, but He just smiles
Because He knows me best.

Jung is my husband.

El Roi – The God Who Sees Me

I picked up a whole chestnut
Fallen to the forest floor,
Still complete in its harsh, prickly case,
Each spike designed to repel and be left alone;
Kept it in my pocket
And took it home.
Each day I looked at it,
Nurtured it, kept it warm,
Noticed it, until it started to crack.
There, to my amazement,
A cross-shaped split at the base –
Gradually expanding and opening from a central point,
Its cactus-like thorns bowing to dried fragility –
Started to open up,
Revealing a pale soft skin
Inner lining of comfort and velvet;
A split and uncovering of shiny brown core
Brought to the surface,
Emerging into light
With a smooth kernel softly gleaming.

Are we like this, Lord?
So hostile to Your love, a response that intentionally
Silences Your words, shuns Your touch, avoids Your gaze?
I can do it myself, am independent, don't need a 'crutch';
I'll live life my way.
I tried that once

In a time of crisis:
Blamed God and turned away,
Mixed with the world, followed its lead,
But as Cat Stevens would sing at the time,
"Oh baby, baby, it's a wild world
and it's hard to get by just upon a smile."*

You, Lord, are always there
Beckoning, available, inviting us
To join You in a Love, Peace and Joy
That is not of this world;
All-consuming and passionately jealous for us,
And You waited for me,
Tenderly holding out Your arms,
Father to child, with mutual joy.

* *'Wild World' by Cat Stevens from the album 'Tea for the Tillerman'; 1970; Songwriter: Yusuf Islam; Wild World lyrics © BMG Rights Management, Royalty Network.*

He Drew a Heart

I saw a hand with a pen.
I watched the hand
And it slowly drew a heart shape.
I looked up to see who was drawing,
Saw the image of Jesus' face,
His wonderful enigmatic smile;
Such an accepting, gracious, merciful, overwhelming smile
That only He can do.
He handed me the piece of paper
And said, "You are very loved."
He didn't use words,
But said it all with His eyes and smile
And the way He personally handed the paper to me.
He gave me the paper to keep;
Yes, Jesus handed me a piece of paper
With a heart on it
He had drawn
Which says,
You are loved,
Loved by Me.

Seaward

It looks very inviting; compelling first steps
Into dry sand, easy shallow footprints;
Powdery soft sand, light, carefree,
Pleasant, wiggling tickled toes.

Then into dense, soaked, golden sand;
Heavy-going, slurpy, waterlogged, damp,
Rippled furrows, shells, seaweed strands,
Little crabs, worm casts, bubbles, enjoying.

Into the shallows; paddling, chilly ankles,
Pausing, paddling, kicking, splashing,
Massaging rhythmic waves, pleasing,
Sinking, moving, pleasure, smiling.

Into the deep; uninhibited, wet, cold,
Fun, adventurous, exciting, laughing,
Surprised, toppling, soaked, brine-tasting,
Enveloped, floating, exhilarating, free.

Based on Ezekiel 47:3-5.

Coming Down the Ski Lift

I'm sitting here
Not only feeling foolish, embarrassed,
But aggrieved.
I should be skiing down,
Feel the icy wind slap my face,
Surge of excitement as I propel my poles forward,
Ready for the adrenaline rush
Of pristine mountain snow
Conquered by me
Into furrows and spray –
But I wasn't allowed.
So now I sit
Coming down in the chair lift,
Head hung low, eyes downcast,
Skis drooping, unused poles across my lap;
Overwhelming disappointment,
Wasted hopes, at a loss.
Why? Why me? Why now?

We have all thought this, Lord,
When our prayers seem unanswered,
When we feel let down;
Yes, when we feel let down by You.
Surely we ask for what's right, what's best for us?
Yet it doesn't happen
The way we want, the way we thought it would be,
And that effects us deeply. Where are You, God?

Are You listening?
Have I done something wrong
That You cannot obey my prayer,
That You do not answer it my way,
That You ignore my solutions?

Or are You protecting me in an unseen way
That I will never know?

I have never skied! This was a picture during a prayer time.

Will You Come, Follow Me?

Disciples were called and they all did.
The rich man invited, resisted.
Bartimaeus was healed and he did so.
A leper desired, was dismissed though.

And what about you, is He asking?
Are you ignoring Him? Just multitasking?
An adventure awaits.
Stop juggling those plates;
Why not turn around, follow the Master?

Snowfall

We are under the snow cloud,
No gusty breeze to sweep aside;
Bridal white flakes falling, falling, falling,
Teaspoons of crystal,
Bleached moths descending
So gently, so quietly.
Follow just one as it twirls and dances among the others,
Incessantly diving onto any shed, hedge or tree
To smother and cover it
In an icy foam.
A burst pillow of feathers
Scattering, playing, pervading
Our senses;
Bowed every bough of drooping conifer,
Surrendered and engaged;
Such monochrome beauty.

This day I do not desire Colour, but
Just to catch a snowflake on my tongue.

Supermarket Flowers

I bought some tulips,
"Reduced" near the checkout,
To brighten up the windowsill.
Cups of flame, tall and erect,
Each responded to the warmth and the light
And spread their petals like a lotus,
An emerging sunset within each one.
Today they have faded and drooped;
Petals fall off at the merest touch.
Time to be discarded
But... look again
At the exposed vivid green stigma:
Dusty navy blue stamens still scattering pollen.
They opened ripe for pollination;
Are they disappointed that
No bee or butterfly came?
Yet I have treasured them,
Admired them,
Investigated them closely with a magnifying glass,
Photographed their exquisite arrangement, colours and
    textures.
They brought me joy;
I've pondered the wonder of them;
I hope that is enough.

Poem for the Queen

I wonder if, as she lay in those last few moments,
She looked out on the purple heather
And watched the midday shadows pass across the crags;
She knew her time was passing...
And slipped gently away into the valley,
Closing her eyes to the last of her duties
With completion and dignity.
Her book is closed on earth
But in God's book a page is just turning,
Opening with her name 'Elizabeth',
For that is how she came into our world, 'pledged to God'.
She leaves the world a better place
Than if she had not been with us.
But we're a nation not ready to be dressed in black.

NB. the meaning of the name 'Elizabeth' in Hebrew is 'pledged to God'. (Written September 2022.)

Sweet Peas

Sweet Pea seeds need to be nicked and soaked
Even before you hope to see them germinate;
Those first two seed leaves
Ushering in full growth
Of the most fragrant and beautifully delicate flowers.

Lord, in my vicinity,
Are there hard nuts to crack?
Hearts to be softened,
Even before the light of Christ can enter in?

I have 18 pots of seedlings for planting,
Nurtured over winter in the greenhouse;
Tended, buds nipped, intertwined tendrils lovingly untangled,
They are prepared ready for growth and exuberant life.

In my square container, I drill holes that water may course
    free,
Lay a base layer with soft silver grey slate.
(Is that slate from rain-drenched Welsh mountains?
I went to a slate mine once...)
I caress it, stroke it, make a mosaic pattern,
Then cover with clattery pea shingle,
Each stone unique in colouring, size and shape,
Rough to touch, dirty, unattractive but useful,
And pour over dark moist compost...
There are thousands of organisms,

Pin-head small micro nutrients captured in this warm crumble
    mix.

Father, may I lay a firm porous foundation
That Your life-giving Spirit pours through me;
May I be a bed of rich soil
That You grow in
So that those in my vicinity may see Christ in me
And are ready to be moved into a new pot
Of faith and commitment.

My tray of plants call out, "Choose me!
I am strong and will succeed!
I am weak and small but will thrive!"
I place old beech branches for the wigwam,
For these little ones to anchor and know their support.

Lord, who in my vicinity feels weak,
Insignificant, overlooked, small and needs Your strength,
Your faithfulness, Your stability?
They need to witness my strength and my faithfulness –
My stability.

An expert said to plant salvias in between
To prevent a disease,
So I have sown salvia seeds in two 'pause' lines
In the centre of my container.

Lord, all is ready,
Plants selected,

Tied to the support,
Drenched with water,
The wigwam rises high above.

Lord, only You can make them grow;
I am a gardener
But You are creator
Of spirit.

You have prepared the fertile ground long ago;
May I sow, tend and nurture, provide support
So that souls thrive and grow
And become full-flowered scented beauty for You,
Reaching up high to the heavens.

Kimmeridge

Ungainly walk over cobbles;
A secluded platform,
Noughts and crosses etched;
Low tide revealing tropical rock pools,
Vivid feather seaweed, tiny ruby crusted shells;
Sea green lapping and caressing.
A lazy afternoon painting and resting;
Above all, Flavell's tower,
Colonnaded lookout observatory,
Perched on perilous slope,
Stagnant amongst the beaten rock,
Crumbling shale, wandering waves.
A firm foundation is Jesus Christ our Lord;
He will never be shaken.

Dorset Psalm

My heart sings by the Jurassic coast; gazing at vast rhythmic waves, sea blue jewels of platinum, turquoise, azure and sapphire, fresh salty air, softest Shell Bay sand, silver Chesil pebbles, etched Kimmeridge ledge, Durdle's limestone arch, Bradstock's yellow ochre cliffs...

My heart melts at marshmallow sunrises and blood orange sunsets rippling gold towards my feet, rolling crumpled quilts of patchwork green fields, corrugated ploughing, ric-rac hedgerows, misty lilac hills...

My heart smiles with Dorset dialect, warm apple cake, blue vinney cheese, thatched pubs, Branksome barbecues, Arne Dartford warblers, spiral Dorset buttons, intricate feather stitchery, extravagant folk music, Hardy's melancholy poems...

There is a longing within me – is it nostalgia? Is it more? A calling back?
An Hireath?
Did Columba mourn for Ireland?
Did Aidan grieve for Iona?

Would it be the same if we returned?
Annual holidays are uplifting, joyous, delightful, visiting dearest friends, revisiting favourite places and discovering new ones

But...

Would the effort, change, upheaval, disruption of our 35 years
    here be worth it just for me, a selfish indulgence not relevant
    to my family?

Or does the memorable beauty and nostalgic heritage enable
    me to truly love and treasure wherever I am placed?
Did my gentle coastal upbringing there in Dorset instil in me
    gifts of encircling creation, beauty, stillness, contentment, a
    foothold, that I can bring to wherever I am placed?

Are You calling me back, Lord, or do I remain here to settle
    into this place, and instead surrender more of myself to You
    – for I want You to have my heart and to be my treasure.
Lord, I want You to hold my heart
And not be entrapped in a place of memories.

Confession

Sinless.
Father, it is a word that does not come
Easily upon the lips,
Yet that is who I am.
And if I deny Christ's perfect sacrifice –
His blood, His pain, His anguish,
His victory and triumph –
Then I deny the right
To call myself 'sinless'.
For that is who I am.
Granted the most marvellous and wondrous freedom
From all my body craves me to be,
From all the devil tempts me to be,
From all the world deceives me to be,
From all the confusion and emotion
Of living in this dark earth;
Your light has come and searched for me
And found me.
I reach up in Your beam
And I am swathed in brilliance and purity –
Sinless,
Set free,
By Grace
At this moment of confession.

Song

*(for when you cannot feel God's presence
or are unsure of His Love for you)*

How can I be certain His love for me is real?
How can I go on and face the world the way I feel?
How can I imagine His arms surrounding me?
How can I feel safe, secure, unlimited and free?

This is Love, no boundaries round it;
This is Love, so purifying;
This is Love, no hiding from it;
This is Love.

How can I remember the promises You made?
How can I recall the words of Scripture as they fade?
How can I put on my mask, say everything's okay,
When pain and hurt confuses me, each and every day?

This is Love, no boundaries round it;
This is Love, so purifying;
This is Love, no hiding from it;
This is Love.

I am always with you, and I claim you as My own;
All around are family, you need not be alone;
Come and walk beside Me, and place your hand in Mine;

I am your security, Relationship Divine.

This is Love, no boundaries round it;
This is Love, so purifying;
This is Love, no hiding from it;
This is Love.

Healing Ministry

Empty me from worldly stain
To enter in Your throne room reign.
Awe and wonder, thanks and praise;
On You, O Lord, I rest my gaze.

Spirit, fill my language now
As beneath the Crown I bow.
Disquiet my tongue its frantic pace;
Give mercy as I seek Your face.

May Your Voice bring tears of hope;
Restore, inspire new ways to cope.
I place my hands to reach for You;
My demeanour honours You.

Pour out Your Spirit more on me,
Your power and authority;
See blind eyes open, deaf ears hear,
Arthritis numbed and cancers healed.

Depressions lifted, lost returned,
Reconciliation birthed;
Grief is comforted, infections calmed,
MND knows Jesus' balm.

May all these know a lighter touch
For seekers here have carried much;

Freshness, clarity and peace
In healing ministry relief.

Written for Acorn Christian Healing Foundation 40th Anniversary 2023.

I Give You Permission

Inspire me, judge me, redefine me,
Strengthen, build and fortify me,
Hue me, prune me, redesign me,
Captivate and purify me.
Teach me well, disciple me,
Keep me in humility;
Let my tongue a servant be,
My heart enlarged for poverty.

Verdley Woods

Coniferous or deciduous...
Both have their beauty
Either side of this forest path.
One exuberantly golden, over which buzzards glide and call;
Flourishing wildlife retreat from our steps.
The other tall, slender, straight, serene,
Pruned purposefully for timber.
Both in quiet,
Bathed in dappled sunshine.
Which do you prefer?

We have so many choices:
Brown or white?
Marmite or peanut butter?
Left or right?
Belief or not?
Which do you prefer?

But before you've decided,
Just linger a while.
Think *why* you prefer it.
Have you really considered the alternative?
Investigate, research, experience, explore and taste
And then,
Only then, make your final decision
Whether to believe
Or not.

The Kench

Just a five-minute walk
To the sound of waders and trickling water's edge,
Mudflats and salt marsh,
Purslane and glasswort, samphire, sea asters,
Chirruping of crickets,
Warm smell of old litter
Marooned by the morning's gentle tide,
Sheer wild flatland beauty,
A rippling clear blue lagoon
Perfectly reflecting a long-necked egret,
Cries of curlew and gull,
Soft glistening mud hiding creatures in its depths.
Such peace and tranquillity.
A nature reserve – rangers protecting, caring, loving;
And I'm fully appreciating.

Lee on Solent

Father, it is warm here
Away from the bracing wind of the foreshore,
Stepped back in the sun
And the gentle breeze,
Able to be comfortable and observe
Without interruption or noise.
People taking leisure and pleasure
Just sitting idly, walking dogs,
Watching the sail boats and France-destined ferries,
Listening to the buffeting of jet skis
And whirring sea rescue helicopters.
Shuffled footsteps of elderly women
Remembering their grandchildren
And reminiscing 1950s holidays,
Entering their retirement home by the sea – newly built and
    inviting.
Quick purposeful steps of a waitress
Returning for the afternoon shift.
Couples separated into male and female,
Full of male and female conversations.
All manner of boats – colourful Isle of Wight shuttles, cruising
    yachts, billowing dinghies,
A lone angler, patiently waiting as only they know how,
People peering through binoculars,
A view of Ryde's parish church,
Renews romantic memories of visits many years ago...
Gliders elegantly swooping – eagles of the sky,

Swiftly ebbing sea, sparkling and shimmering like diamond
    facets in a spotlight,
A shack with punnets of cockles, vinegared and peppered.
An overload of the senses.
I have to write it down…

Thank You for the gift of Time.
Let us cradle it, absorb it, relish it and consume it
Just like this shellfish on my little wooden fork.

Golgotha

We see the dark clouds forming,
The foreboding rain and gloom
Scudding all too quickly towards us,
Masking the blue sky.
We fear and are bowed low,
But there is the Cross on the hill –
Strong, magnificent and powerful –
Between you and the clouds.
Look to the cross, not the clouds;
Focus on the nearness of Jesus,
Not the issues beyond your control.

Biskey Howe

I need first to set the scene:

It is evening... sitting on Biskey Howe viewpoint; stunning, exactly what I was searching for in the Lake District. Sun is so warm. All is serene and calm. Smudged fells fading with the sun's rays, but others deepening with shadow and gentle peaks. Love the little pot of pretty purple pansies placed on a stone. A lone boat on the platinum lake, muted hills sleeping against one another like a lamb to its mother, nestled, snuggled for warmth. Deep furrows and ridges, velvet smooth then craggy. Broccoli trees tumble to the shore. Sun refuses to dip, continues to paint everything vivid lime, copper and forest green. Majestic creation crafted by an artistic hand, moulded by beauty, grown with empathy.

I felt these words in my spirit and wrote them down...

"Be still, be at peace,
All is calm;
You are safe in My arms.
My countenance is with you.
I relish the time you spend with Me.
You can count on Me for everything;
Reach out and touch Me
For I am very close beside you.
Feel My breath; feel My touch; feel My love surrounding you
As the mountains surround the lake.
I am strong rock all around you;

I am firm foundation;
I am height and depth;
I am sun and cloud;
I am sunrise and sunset;
I am birdsong and silence;
I am lavish and sparse;
I am distant yet near;
I am all to you,
Precious child."

Psalm 23 and a Half

My phone is my companion, it never leaves my side.
I sit in silence, stare at it, a mesmerising guide.
I must admit there's some good apps, enlarging my
    perspective,
And there's all kinds of Christian input to promote the life that
    I live.
I keep in touch with family, friends' news and prayer requests.
An early morning 'Wordle' is the game I like the best.
I stack up all the selfies, and check the times of trains;
Remember *Yellow Pages*? Well, we won't see those again.
Audio books and YouTube crafts, easy holiday booking;
Scrolling through locations, with evenings spent 'just looking'.
It leads me to all kinds of films and mails and blogs and posts,
Entranced by sponsored adverts to just buy, not count the cost.
It makes me laugh with videos of cats and comedy scenes;
I follow adventurous families to discover where they've been.
It seems to be unaware of what is right and what is wrong
And can tantalise my senses to a place I don't belong.
It influences life so much and takes up so much time;
Has it given me joy, or distracted me and actually been a bind?
I really just don't need it demanding my attention;
More updates or worrying scams just increases hypertension.
Even when I'm ill or dying, it bleeps and buzzes and pings,
And only then is it laid aside with all my other things.
So while I have the chance, I'm going to leave it on the shelf,
And walk and talk and sing and dance, explore just by myself.

That's when I'll find quiet waters, and green fields to rest my
  head
And listen to the Father's words; and not do what Google said.

Diagnosis

He does this every day.
Scans through his notes,
Turns his swivel chair
And looks at me
With warm, compassionate eyes,
And says,
"We've found a lump."
He always waits
In the silence
For
The shock,
The fear,
The tears;
Waits
Till he is ready for the next stage:
Prognosis.
Questions,
Treatment,
Hope, despair, anxiety, sadness.
Out the door I go
And another enters in.
He does this every day.
He does this every day.
A life-saver
Or soft harbinger of death,
Every day presiding over
Another file,

Another person,
Another future.
He does this every day.
He does this every day.
All day.

Just Sitting

"Sometimes I sits and thinks
And sometimes I just sits…"
Said Winnie the Pooh.
I'm just sitting
On this bench on a hot March day;
"Unusual for this time of year,"
The weather presenters exclaim.
Behind me, the crisp rust leaves of the beech hedge
Rustle like cellophane and shudder in the soft breeze.
Before me, the newly opened magnolia
Reveals its virgin buds, spreading wide each pearlescent cup
As if a ballerina with flourishing pirouette.
In the distance, the vibrant forsythia –
Sumptuously bright yellow splatters against the clear azure
    sky.
Beneath me, almost inconspicuous violets
Hide their delicate beauty within protective heart-shaped
    leaves;
And clumps of lemon cream primroses,
Joyous communities, faces upturned to welcome the day.
And I,
I am sitting here
With my Lord beside me.
Sometimes we talk
And sometimes we just sit.
We listen to the robin's sweet song

As it cautiously edges nearer and puffs out its crimson chest
   with each warble;
No symphony matches this.
My neighbour hand feeds them with mealworms
So he'll probably head off there.
Two buzzards call overhead, soaring, chasing, defending, and
   disappear;
We like that.
Occasionally I pray-talk,
Ask for people, ask for me;
But mostly we just sit,
Breathe in the air, wallow in the warmth, rest in the silence;
We like that.
Woodpigeons flap and flounder overhead;
An unseen great tit shouts *teach-er! teach-er!* from the holly
   tree;
No doubt he hears a call from his mate.
Sometimes, Jesus and I, we sit and think,
And sometimes we just sit;
We like that.

Also by Linda Daruvala

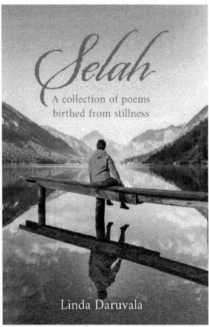

Selah

ISBN 781788156103

Selah is a Hebrew word that appears in many of the biblical psalms. It is an instruction to the listener to pause and reflect on what has just been sung.

This spiritually nourishing collection of poetry was written as Linda Daruvala paused and reflected on Christian retreats and in places of stillness. From poetic paintings of God's creation to a Psalm-like outpouring of her heart to God, Linda echoes the experiences and emotions that are common to many of us in our journey with the Lord.

Available from all good bookshops, or scan the QR code to buy a copy from the publisher.

www.onwardsandupwards.org/product/selah